BLOOMFIELD TOWNSHIP PUBLIC LIBRARY

3 1160 00451 5206

P9-CRC-718

BLOOMFIELD TOWNSHIP PUBLIC LIBRARY
1099 Lone Pine Road
Bloomfield Hills, MI 48302-2410

Common Colds

Dr. Alvin Silverstein,

Virginia Silverstein, and

Laura Silverstein Nunn

BLOOMFIELD TOWNSHIP PUBLIC LIBRARY
1099 Lone Pine Road
Bloomfield Hills, MI 48302-2410

My Health

Franklin Watts

A Division of Grolier Publishing

New York • London • Hong Kong • Sydney

Danbury, Connecticut

Photographs ©: Custom Medical Stock Photo: 12, 29 right; Monkmeyer Press: 24 (Ullmann); NASA: 7; Photo Researchers: 35 (Michael P. Gadomski), 20 (GRANTPIX), 33 (Aaron Haupt), 4 (Ken Lax), 38 (Will & Deni McIntyre), 26 (Blair Seitz), 8 (SPL), 36 (John Watney/SS); PhotoEdit: 6 (Mary Kate Denny), 31 (Michael Newman), 37 (Mark Richards), 39 (D. Young-Wolff); Superstock, Inc.: 18, 27, 32; Tony Stone Images: 22 (David Leach), 9 (LSHTM), 29 left (Vincent Oliver), 19 (Frank Siteman), 34 (Don Smetzer); Visuals Unlimited: 11 (David M. Phillips).

Medical illustration by Leonard Moragn
Cartoons by Rick Stromoski

Visit Franklin Watts on the Internet at:
http://publishing.grolier.com

Library of Congress Cataloging-in-Publication Data

Silverstein, Alvin.
    Common Colds / by Alvin Silverstein, Virginia Silverstein, and Laura Silverstein Nunn.
        p.   cm.—(My Health)
    Includes bibliographical references and index.
    Summary: Explains how people catch colds, how the body fights the germs, how colds are spread, and what precautions people can take against them.
      ISBN 0-531-11579-8 (lib. bdg.)   0-531-16410-1 (pbk.)
      1. Cold (Disease)—Juvenile literature.   [1. Cold (Disease) 2. Diseases.]
I. Silverstein, Virginia B. II. Nunn, Laura Silverstein. III. Title. IV. Series.
RF361.S554   1999
616.2'05—dc21   98-22025
                                       CIP
                                       AC

© 1999 Dr. Alvin Silverstein, Virginia Silverstein, and Laura Silverstein Nunn
All rights reserved. Published simultaneously in Canada.
Printed in the United States of America
1 2 3 4 5 6 7 8 9 10 R 08 07 06 05 04 03 02 01 00 99

Contents

JUL 1 2 2000

Everybody Catches Colds!

Ah-choo! You know that miserable feeling. In fact, you may be having it right now. Your nose is so stuffed up, you can't breathe. You're coughing. You feel hot and tired and just plain awful!

Doctors call colds "common colds" because they happen so often, and to so many people. In fact, chances are that you or someone you know has had a cold in the past 2 weeks.

Kids catch more colds than anybody else. Babies may have as many as nine colds in their first year of life. As we get older, we catch fewer colds. But parents and teachers catch a lot of colds, too. They catch them from children!

Did You Know...

You can expect to have from 50 to 100 colds in your lifetime.

◀ **Nobody likes having a cold. A cold can make you sneeze, cough, and have a runny nose.**

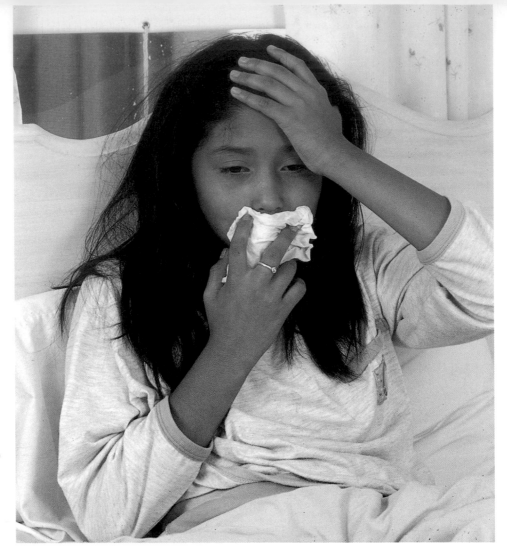

Have you ever stayed home from school because you had a cold?

Colds are not very dangerous. People usually get better in about a week, even if they don't take any medicine. But colds can make us feel really bad. People miss more days of school and work because of colds than for all other diseases combined!

Why do we catch more colds when it is cold outside? In cold weather, people stay inside with the doors and windows closed and spend a lot of time with other people. This makes it easier for colds to move from one person to another. You can catch a cold in the summer, too. And in tropical places, where it is hot all the time, people catch a lot of colds. They catch the most colds when it is rainy. Can you guess why?

What causes colds? What can you do to feel better when you have a cold? Let's find out more about them.

Even Astronauts Catch Colds

The *Apollo 9* space mission in 1969 couldn't take off on time because all three astronauts on the crew had colds. Blast-off had to wait a week until they all got better. In 1990, it happened again. The commander of the Atlantis Space Shuttle couldn't fly because his nose was too stuffed up. Waiting a week until he got better cost more than $2 million!

James A. McDivitt (left), David R. Scott (center), and Russell L. Schweickart (right) all had colds on the day *Apollo 9* **was scheduled to take off.**

What Is a Cold?

A common cold is an illness that causes a stuffed-up, runny nose and a sore throat. It is caused by very tiny germs called **viruses.**

Viruses cannot live by themselves. They can live only inside a living animal or plant. The viruses that

Strange Ideas

Hippocrates, an ancient Greek doctor, lived nearly 2,500 years ago.

Before people knew about viruses and other germs, they had some strange ideas about what caused illnesses. An ancient Greek doctor named Hippocrates thought that colds were caused by waste matter in the brain. When the waste overflowed, he said, it ran out the nose.

In the Middle Ages, people thought illnesses were due to demons. They said that sneezing was very dangerous because a person's soul might be sneezed out, and a demon could sneak in and replace it. Saying "God bless you!" when people sneezed was a way to protect them from demons.

cause colds can live in the soft, wet lining inside a person's nose and throat. More than 200 different kinds of viruses can cause colds.

Viruses are much too small to see. In fact, you can't even see a virus with a magnifying glass or a typical microscope. Scientists need special **electron microscopes** to see a virus. Nobody even knew viruses existed until about 100 years ago.

How small is a virus? Picture this. If a virus were as big as an ant, then you would be as big as the whole Earth!

Viruses are tiny. These cold viruses have been magnified more than 500,000 times.

Activity I: Making a Virus Model

Scientists with powerful electron microscopes have found that one kind of cold virus looks like the picture shown on page 9. You can make a model of a cold virus, using modeling clay.

Medical Words About Colds

Some cold viruses are called **rhinoviruses**. "Rhino" comes from the Greek word for "nose." A stuffed-up, runny nose is called **rhinitis**. "Rhinoceros" comes from the same Greek word. When your nose is stuffed up with a cold, it may feel as big as a rhino's nose!

Cold viruses need to be inside people to make more cold viruses. They get inside the cells in the lining of the nose and throat and turn cells into virus-making factories. When a cell is full of viruses, it bursts open and the viruses spill out. The viruses are carried out of the body in the wet, slimy liquid that drips out. When you cough or sneeze, tiny droplets of liquid spray out and carry viruses with them.

10

The Body Defends Itself

The body has many defenses against germs. Cold viruses that get into the mouth may be swept into the tonsils, where **white blood cells** are on patrol. Like good soldiers, the white cells surround the germs and destroy them. Other viruses are swallowed. When they get down into the stomach, they are destroyed in a pool of acid.

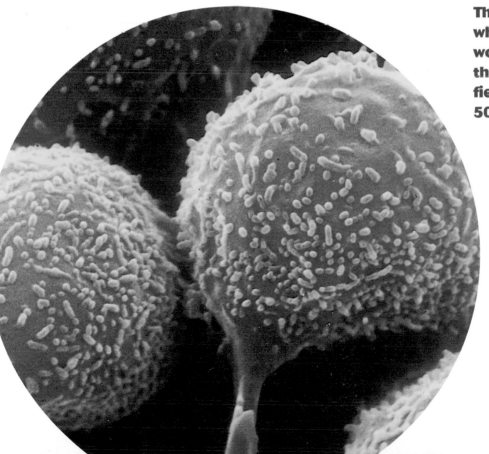

This is what your white blood cells would look like if they were magnified more than 50,000 times.

The nose also has defenses against invading germs. Germs ride on dust particles and drops of liquid, which may be trapped by the bristly hairs inside the nostrils. The germs that sneak past these hairs fall into the gooey fluid that covers the lining of the nose. This fluid is called **mucus**. The fluid flows along the lining, carrying the trapped germs toward the back of the throat. Then they may be swallowed. But the mucus does not move as fast when the air is cold and dry. Some viruses grab onto the outside of the cells and squirt some of their chemicals inside. These chemicals hold the instructions for making new cold viruses.

Viruses use the materials inside living cells to make more viruses. This rhinovirus is magnified more than 900,000 times.

What Is that Gooey Stuff?

Just what is that gooey stuff that drips out of your nose when you have a cold? It is made up of mucus, plus fluid that leaked out of blood vessels in the lining of the nose. It contains viruses and other germs as well as dust particles that were trapped in the mucus. As the body fights the cold virus, the fluid in the nose also contains the remains of dead lining cells and the bodies of white blood cells that were killed in the battle. There may also be a bit of blood as the lining of the nose gets cracked and sore. Around the fourth day, the yucky stuff turns green or yellow from all the dead blood cells.

The cells that were invaded call for help. They use chemicals to call for the body's defenders. Some of the chemicals warn nearby cells about the viruses and help to protect them. Other chemicals call white blood cells. Still others make the lining of the nose leaky, so that the defending white blood cells can swim in more easily.

These body defenses help to protect us against viruses, but they also cause some of the things that make us feel so miserable. The leaky lining gets swollen, and there is less room for air to flow in and out. So it gets even harder to breathe. The extra mucus dribbles out, producing a runny nose. When particles get caught on the nose hairs, the brain sends a message to the chest muscles and we **sneeze**. Some of the extra mucus that drips down the back of the throat irritates it and makes us **cough**. Some of the chemicals sent out by the damaged cells make the brain increase the body temperature, producing **fever**.

Some of the white blood cells produce special chemicals called **antibodies.** They fit the virus, just as a key fits into a lock. Antibodies may kill germs, or they may make it easier for

Did You Know...

When you sneeze, air explodes out of your lungs at a speed of 100 miles (160 kilometers) per hour. The air in a cough travels at 500 miles (805 km) per hour!

AcHoo!

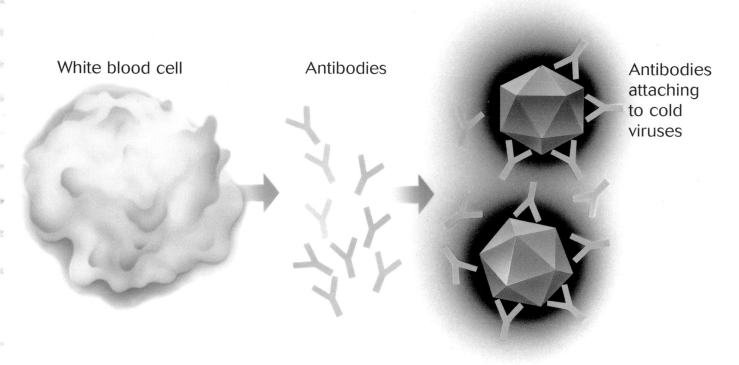

White blood cell Antibodies Antibodies attaching to cold viruses

When viruses invade your body, some white blood cells produce antibodies. The antibodies attach to the viruses and help destroy them.

white blood cells to eat them. Once the body has made antibodies against the cold virus, it keeps some copies even after the cold is over. They will be ready to fight if the same kind of virus invades you again.

So, if you are protected by antibodies, why can you still catch more colds? Because there are more than 200 kinds of cold viruses, and the antibodies don't work on most of them. Older people get fewer colds than children because they have fought off more cold viruses and are protected against them.

Diary of a Cold

Day 1

I found a new home! My old home sneezed out some viruses. They landed on her toy truck, and then her brother grabbed it. The viruses got on his hands, and then he picked his nose. Quickly my viruses dug in. Some of them settled into nice wet cells. There was plenty of food there for them. Soon the cells were making more viruses. Uh-oh! The burglar alarms are going off. The soldiers are coming. My virus army is in for a fight!

Day 2

I think we're winning. Things are very uncomfortable, though. Some of my viruses were drowned. Others were poisoned or "eaten" by those enemy soldiers. But we have them outnumbered, and we keep on making more viruses.

Day 3

It's getting hot in here, and the soldiers keep coming. We've killed a lot of them, though. My home is really complaining. He says his head hurts, and his throat hurts, and his nose is so stuffy he can hardly breathe. I wish he'd stop whining.

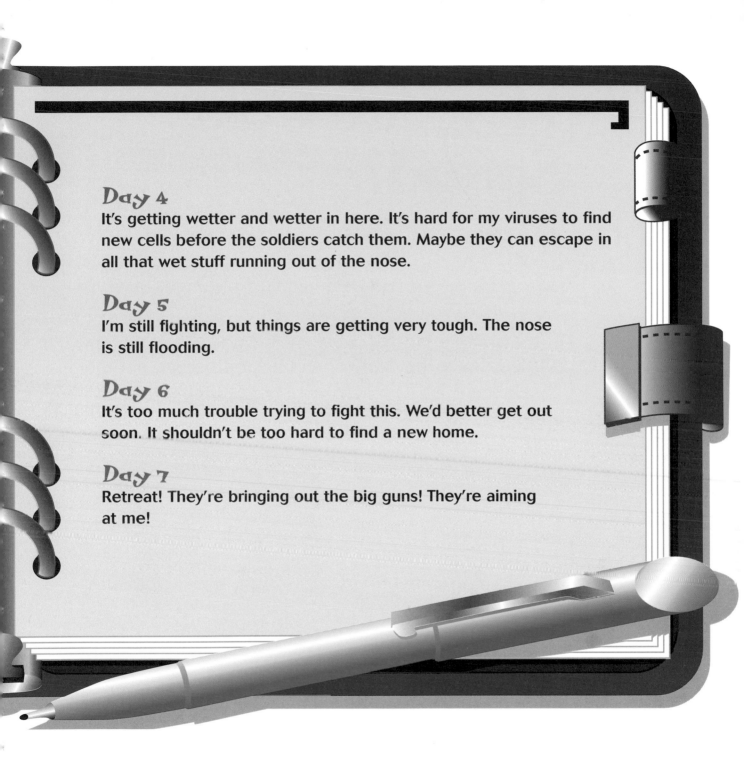

Day 4

It's getting wetter and wetter in here. It's hard for my viruses to find new cells before the soldiers catch them. Maybe they can escape in all that wet stuff running out of the nose.

Day 5

I'm still fighting, but things are getting very tough. The nose is still flooding.

Day 6

It's too much trouble trying to fight this. We'd better get out soon. It shouldn't be too hard to find a new home.

Day 7

Retreat! They're bringing out the big guns! They're aiming at me!

How Are Colds Spread?

If you have a cold, you might know where you got it—maybe you were playing with a friend who had been sick for a day or two. Then again, you might have no idea where you got your cold.

Colds are spread from one person to another. Viruses leave the body of an infected person and get inside the body of a healthy person.

Blast from the Past

Ben Franklin slept with his windows open because he believed that fresh air prevents colds. He was right. Fresh air spreads out the virus particles in the air, making it less likely that you will breathe them in.

Benjamin Franklin

Cold viruses can spread when people share food or drinks.

When you get sick, virus particles are hiding out in the fluid in your eyes, nose, and throat. But how do these viruses leave your body and find a new home in somebody else's body? Some scientists think cold viruses spread through the air. When you sneeze or cough—or even when you talk—tiny droplets of moisture spray out of your nose and mouth. Cold viruses can ride on those tiny droplets. If you have to cough, turn your face away from your friends so they won't catch your germs.

You can catch a cold by touching an object, such as a telephone, that a sick person had touched.

Some scientists say that colds are spread by hands. If you rub your eyes or wipe your nose when you are sick, you can get cold viruses on your hands. Then if you touch somebody else's hand, you pass on some of your cold germs. According to these scientists, you can also catch a cold by touching something that was recently touched by someone with a cold. Cold viruses can survive for hours on things like doorknobs, telephones, dishes, books, toys, and money.

Activity 2:
See How Viruses Spread

Put some liquid vegetable dye in a bowl. (Use wild colors like purple, blue, or green.) Dip your fingers in the bowl to wet them with the dye. Now do some normal things, like eating a snack or bouncing a ball or drawing a picture. Every few minutes, dip your fingers in the bowl with the dye again.

After 15 minutes, look at yourself in a mirror. How many times did you touch your face? You'll be able to tell because you will have colored spots from the vegetable dye on your skin. What else did you touch?

You probably didn't realize how often you touch your face without even thinking about it. Now can you imagine how hard it is to keep from spreading cold germs?

People catch more colds during cold weather. Wearing warm clothes can help you stay healthy.

Has anybody ever told you, "Don't go outside without a jacket—you'll catch cold"? This warning is not exactly true. (Remember, colds are caused by viruses, not by the weather.) But cold weather may make it easier for you to get sick. Cold weather weakens your body's defenses. If you come in contact with cold viruses, your body's white blood cell defenders may be too weak to fight off the infection. It may also be easy to catch a cold when you are too hot, very tired, or if you have not been eating very well.

People who smoke cigarettes may have worse colds than non-smokers. Children of parents who smoke tend to have more colds, and other health problems, too. Pollution and allergies also put a heavy load on the defenses in your nose and throat and may lead to really bad colds. In general, the more stress you have, the greater your chances are of getting a cold.

The Monday Blues

People get more colds on Mondays than on any other day. Could it be that we just do not want to go to school or to work on Mondays? Well, maybe. But remember, colds take a few days to get started. It takes time for those viruses to multiply. So the cold that you notice on Monday was probably caught the week before, from somebody you met who had a cold.

Playing Cards for Science

Not all scientists agree about how cold germs are spread. In 1986, Dr. Elliot Dick of the University of Wisconsin tried to find out whether cold viruses are spread through the air or by touch. To do this, he asked his students to play card games. A group of healthy students played cards with people who had colds. The students wore big collars so that they

Dr. Dick tried to show that healthy people could catch colds by breathing the same air as people with colds.

couldn't touch their faces. After that card game, more than half of the healthy students got colds. Dr. Dick thought his experiment proved that colds are spread through the air.

In another card game, Dr. Dick gave healthy students cards and poker chips that were covered with mucus and saliva from people with colds. The students didn't want to touch those yucky cards, but they did anyway. Not one of them caught a cold! According to Dr. Dick, this experiment showed that it is not easy to spread cold germs by hand.

Not all scientists agree with Dr. Dick, however. When these scientists did their own experiments, they found that people often caught colds when they touched objects covered with cold germs. Their experiments also showed that it is hard to catch a cold by breathing the air where somebody sneezed.

Don't Put a Cold in Your Pocket

People used to wipe their runny noses on their sleeves. Yuck! Then pocket handkerchiefs were invented. They were a lot neater, but they could still spread colds—especially if you borrowed someone else's handkerchief or if your handkerchief was washed in water that was not hot enough to kill cold viruses. Today we have paper tissues. Use them once, and then throw them away.

People can catch colds from touching objects that have been handled by sick people.

How could these scientists get such different results? Remember, more than 200 different viruses can cause colds. Some viruses travel better through air, and others can survive longer on objects. So people can catch colds either from the air or by touching things, depending on which kinds of cold viruses are going around.

Treating a Cold

What should you do if you have a cold? Are there medications you can take to get better? People go to doctors more for colds than for any other reason. Unfortunately, doctors can't do much for someone with a cold. Of course, there are plenty of cold medicines that you can buy in the supermarket or the drugstore. Medications can make you feel a little better, but they don't fight the viruses that are making you sick.

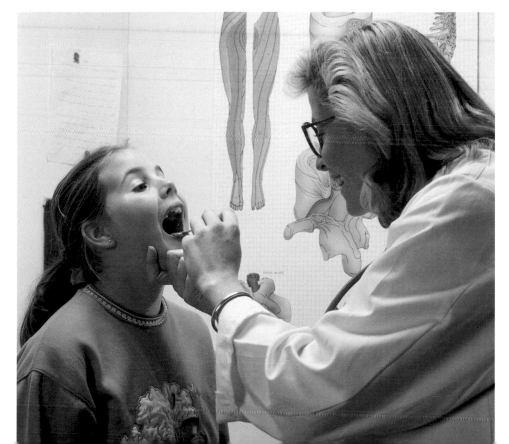

This doctor is examining a girl with a cold.

Some Weird Old Remedies

People have been giving advice about treating colds for a very long time. In ancient Greece, people thought that bleeding could help cure colds. They believed that colds were caused by too much fluid in the body, so doctors actually cut people to help them lose that extra fluid. They also used wormlike leeches to suck the blood of sick people.

Ancient Romans thought you could get rid of a cold by kissing a mouse on its whiskery nose!

During the Middle Ages, Catholics in Europe believed that prayer would cure colds. Garlic necklaces and salted-herring collars were also used to keep away both colds and evil spirits.

Some people ask doctors to give them a shot of penicillin or some other **antibiotic** to get rid of a nasty cold. Antibiotics are good drugs for diseases caused by bacteria, but they do not work on viruses. In fact, taking antibiotics too often may even be harmful, because they may help to breed supergerms that can't be killed by medications.

Aspirin is a popular remedy for treating illnesses like colds—it helps aches and pains and headaches. But not everyone should take aspirin. In the 1970s, scientists found that children who took aspirin for a viral illness were more likely to develop Reye's syndrome, which damages the liver and nervous system. Some even died! Fortunately, Reye's syndrome is very rare. But today, doctors tell parents to give their children acetaminophen (uh-SEE-tuh-MIH-nuh-fuhn) instead of aspirin when they have colds.

▲ Children should not take aspirin to treat a cold.

◀ If a child has a high fever for several days, he or she should see a doctor.

Most people do not need to see a doctor when they have a cold. But some people should. Colds can be very harmful to babies, people older than seventy, pregnant women, and people who have problems with their heart or lungs. These people should call the doctor if:

- cold symptoms are very serious or last for more than a week;
- a child has a fever above 102 degrees Fahrenheit (39 degrees Celsius) for 2 days or more;
- constant coughing keeps a child awake;
- coughing makes colored mucus for more than 2 days;
- bad headaches, stiff neck, swollen glands, or a rash are present.

Colds may sometimes lead to other infections such as **bronchitis, tonsillitis, sinusitis,** ear infections, and **pneumonia**. These are bacterial infections that can develop when the body is weakened by a cold. Unlike viral infections, bacterial infections can be treated with medications.

For most people with colds, the only thing doctors can do is tell them to get some rest, drink plenty of fluids, keep warm, and take over-the-counter drugs to treat cold symptoms. These medications can help dry up a runny nose, stop coughing, and soothe a sore throat and headache.

Some people think that taking extra **vitamin C** and the mineral zinc when cold symptoms first appear may prevent the cold from developing or make it much shorter and milder.

Did You Know...

In the twelfth century, a Jewish philosopher named Maimonides said that chicken soup is good for colds. He may have been right. In 1978, Dr. Marvin Sackner of Mount Sinai Hospital in Miami Beach, Florida, found that chicken soup helped to clear the mucus from a stuffy nose much faster than other liquids.

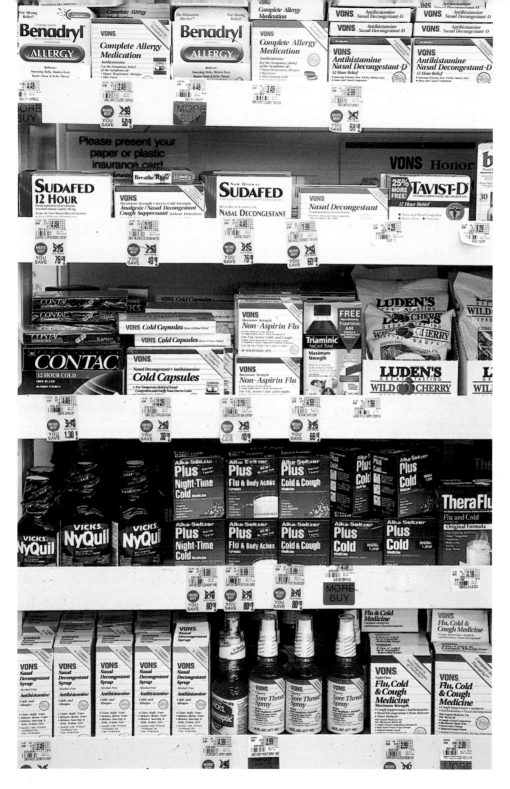

There are dozens of over-the-counter drugs designed to treat cold symptoms.

Preventing Colds

Is it possible to prevent colds? The only sure way to keep from catching a cold is to stay away from people with colds and anything they may have touched. That's not easy. Imagine what your life would be like if you had to stay away from your sick Mom or Dad for a whole week! Or if they had to stay away from you when you

If your Mom and Dad take care of you when you have a cold, they might get sick.

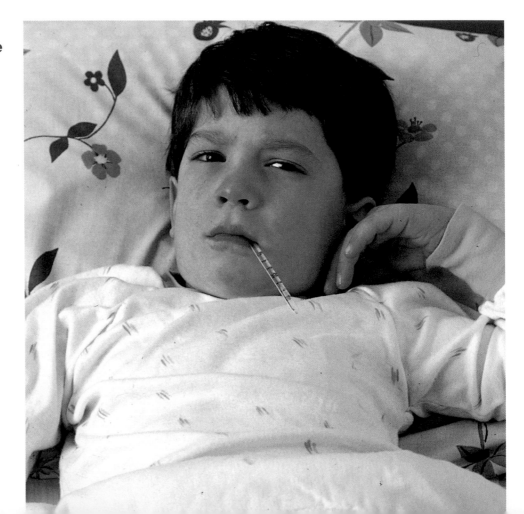

were sick! But there are a few things you can do to prevent colds without having to hide from sick people.

First, you need to cut down the chances for spreading colds. To keep cold viruses from getting to you, try not to touch people who have colds, wash your hands regularly, and always wash your hands before touching your eyes or nose. (Washing your hands won't kill the cold viruses, but it *will* wash them down the drain.) If you are the one with the cold, washing your hands can help keep you from spreading your viruses to others.

The Polite Thing to Do

How many times have you heard, "Cover your mouth when you cough"? Covering your mouth when you cough or sneeze is supposed to be polite. After all, you don't want to send your germs out into the air that other people are breathing. But coughing into your hand leaves germs there—germs that may spread to somebody else through touching. So should you cover or not cover? The best answer: Cover your mouth and then wash your hands!

Washing your hands will get rid of any cold viruses on them.

If you eat well and exercise regularly, you are less likely to catch colds.

Another important way you can keep from catching colds is to stay healthy. You can do this by eating well, exercising regularly, getting enough rest, and practicing clean habits (washing your hands and keeping your body, clothes, food, and dishes clean). If you can keep yourself healthy and strong, then your body's defenses will be strong enough to fight off invading viruses.

Some experts believe that taking vitamin C can help keep your body strong enough to fight off diseases. Other people say you do not need to take extra vitamins because a balanced diet gives you all you need to be healthy. The problem is that you may not always eat what you should.

During the 1980s, Dr. Dick, the researcher you learned about earlier, did some studies on vitamin C.

Oranges and orange juice are good sources of vitamin C.

The Right Way to Blow

Did you know that there is a right way to blow your nose? Experts say that if you blow your nose too hard, you may harm the blood vessels in your nose. You may even force germ-filled mucus into your sinuses or ears, causing bad infections there.

The right way to blow is to hold the tissue in front of your nostrils and blow softly, touching the skin under your nose as little as possible. You're not blowing right if your nose gets all red and sore.

This boy is blowing his nose too hard.

Students were given 2 grams of vitamin C each day for a period of 3 weeks, and then asked to play cards all weekend with sick people. The students who had taken vitamin C did come down with colds, but their symptoms were very mild. They had fewer coughs, and they didn't have to blow their noses as often. Since that study, Dr. Dick has been taking vitamin C to protect himself against colds.

A Cure for Colds?

Many diseases can be knocked out with medications. If you get strep throat, for example, drugs will help kill the bacteria that cause this disease. You may feel a lot better within a few hours after a shot of antibiotic. But not many drugs work against viruses. Besides, by the time you arc starting to feel sick, your body is already fighting off the cold viruses.

Like most drugs, chicken soup does not cure a cold, but it can make you feel better.

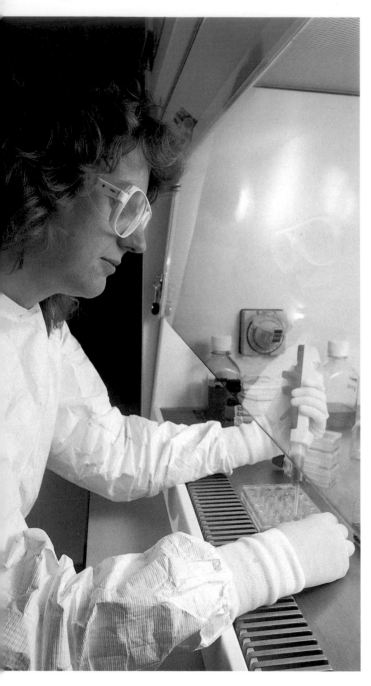

Scientists have learned a lot about cold viruses and how they make us sick. Now they are trying to use some of that knowledge to find ways to protect us from virus attacks.

For example, cold viruses have tiny "hooks" that hold onto special places on the outside of cells in the nose and throat. Once they are firmly attached, the viruses take off their outer coats and slip into the cell. Researchers have found the special places on cells where cold viruses settle down. Now they are working on drugs to block these special spots, so that viruses can't get their hooks into the cells. Scientists are also working on ways to stop viruses from taking off their outer coats so they can slip into the cells.

This scientist is studying viruses.

38

You can get a shot of **vac-cine** to protect yourself from measles, or polio, or chickenpox. Someday, you may be able to get a shot of cold vaccine to keep you from catching colds.

One problem with this idea is that so many different viruses can cause colds. But scientists have found that most of the colds people catch in a particular area are caused by the same type of virus, and that virus stays around for a while. So it may be possible to develop vaccines that will protect people from most of the cold viruses they might be likely to meet during each year's cold season.

Researchers are also trying to find things that different cold viruses have in common, so they can make drugs and vaccines that will work on more than one kind of virus.

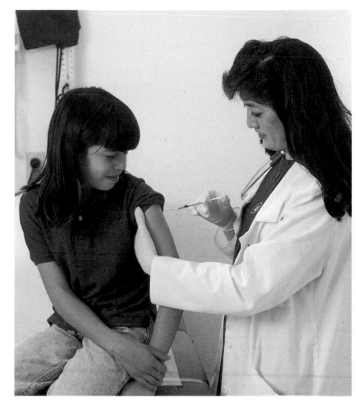

This girl is receiving a shot of vaccine. One day, scientists may develop a vaccine that protects people against some cold viruses.

Glossary

antibiotics—drugs that kill bacteria.

antibodies—special germ-fighting chemicals produced by white blood cells.

bronchitis—an infection of the *bronchi,* the hollow tubes leading from the nose and mouth down into the lungs.

cough—a forceful burst of air from the lungs out through the mouth.

electron microscope—a special kind of microscope that uses beams of electrons (particles with a negative electric charge) rather than light rays to make pictures of very tiny objects.

fever—a body temperature that is higher than normal.

mucus—a gooey liquid produced by cells in the lining of the nose and breathing passages.

pneumonia—an infection of the lungs.

Reye's syndrome—an illness that damages the liver and respiratory system. It may develop when young people with a virus infection take aspirin.

rhinitis—a stuffed-up, runny nose.

rhinovirus—one of the main kinds of viruses that cause colds.

sinusitis—an infection of the lining of the *sinuses*, air-filled spaces inside the bones of the skull.

sneeze—a forceful burst of air from the lungs out through the nose.

tonsillitis—an infection of the *tonsils,* masses of germ-fighting tissue at the back of the throat.

vaccine—a substance that stimulates the body's disease-fighting cells to produce antibodies against a particular kind of germ.

virus—the smallest kind of germ. It cannot even be seen in an ordinary microscope.

vitamin C—a nutrient found in fresh fruits and vegetables that helps to keep the body's disease-fighting cells strong and active.

white blood cell—a disease-fighting cell that travels in the blood and squeezes through the tiny gaps between cells in the body tissues.

Learning More

Books

Benziger, John. *The Corpuscles Meet the Virus Invaders: Fun and Facts About the Common Cold and the Body's Immune System.* Waterville, ME: Corpuscles Intergalactica, 1990.

Demuth, Patricia Brennan. *Achoo!: All About Colds.* New York: Grosset & Dunlap, 1997.

Stille, Darlene R. *The Respiratory System*. Danbury, CT: Children's Press, 1997.

For Advanced Readers

Kittredge, Mary. *The Common Cold.* New York: Chelsea House, 1989.

Murphy, Wendy. *Coping with the Common Cold.* Alexandria, VA: Time-Life Books, 1981.

Pauling, Linus.*Vitamin C and the Common Cold.* San Francisco: W. H. Freeman, 1970.

Stedman, Nancy. *The Common Cold and Influenza.* New York: Julian Messner, 1986.

Organizations and Online Sites
Tips for Online Searches
1. Search for "common cold" (with quotes around the words). If you just look for "cold," you will get a lot of information about cold weather and other cold things.
2. Consider the source of information you find. If a web site belongs to a company that is selling medications for colds, it may not be as objective as a site sponsored by a government agency, medical organization, or university.

The Common Cold
http://shs.sdsu.cdu/healthpro/brochures/commoncold.html
This site has information provided by the San Diego State University Student Health Services.

The Common Cold
http://www.multiplan.com/healthwell/wellness/commoncold.html
This site was developed by the National Institute of Allergy and Infectious Diseases.

How to Survive the Common Cold
http://www.eduplace.com/rdg/gen_act/survival/survive.html
This site has all kinds of activities for kids.

National Institute of Allergy and Infectious Diseases
National Institutes of Health
Bethesda, MD 20892

National Jewish Center for Immunology and Respiratory Medicine
1400 Jackson Street
Denver, CO 80206
Phone: (800) 222-LUNG (Lung Line, provides free advice about respiratory illness)

Surviving the Common Cold
http://www.sb.com/sbhealthcast/pages/cold/cold01.html
This site was developed by SmithKline Beecham, a pharmaceutical company.

Uncommon Remedies for the Common Cold
http://www.kron.com/nc4/healthbeat/stories/2.html
This site was compiled by KRON-TV.

What Is Common about the Common Cold?
http://www.healthfront.com/family/com_cold.htm
This site includes a checklist of cold and flu symptoms.

Index

Page numbers in *italics* indicate illustrations.

About the Authors

Dr. Alvin Silverstein is a Professor of Biology at the College of Staten Island of the City University of New York. **Virginia Silverstein** is a translator of Russian scientific literature. The Silversteins first worked together on a research project at the University of Pennsylvania. Since then, they have produced six children and more than 150 published books for young people.

    Laura Silverstein Nunn, a graduate of Kean College, has been helping with her parents' books since her high school days. She is the coauthor of more than twenty books on diseases and health, science concepts, endangered species, and pets. Laura lives with her husband Matt and their young son Cory in a rural New Jersey town not far from her childhood home.